Wooden Lions

karla k. morton

Texas Review Press
Huntsville, Texas

ACKNOWLEDGEMENTS

Special thanks to the *Writer-In-Resident Grant* from the E2C Foundation which helped bring this book to life, especially the Board: Marsha Dowler, Karen Holland, Cathy Toole, Jane Crews and Robert Davis, also Sherry Londe with Arts in Medicine, as well as the entire community of Seaside, Florida for its generosity and support of so many.

Readings from this book will be set up all across the United States at local and national SPCA's, shelter, rescue and preserve events, fundraisers and facilities, to help protect the innocents.

Some of the poems here have been individually published as follows: "Trout Zen" Connotations Press, "Port Aransas: 2061" Port Aransas Time Capsule, "The Glorious Black" *Hometown, Texas: Young Poets and Artists Celebrate Their Roots* (TCU Press), "Weatherford Cougars" *Langdon Review of the Arts*, "Clowns and Dark Water" Connotations Press, "Singing Doves" *Langdon Review of the Arts*, "Elk Tango" Langdon Review of the Arts, "Leaving Loose the Reigns" Langdon Review of the Arts, "Texas Longhorns" Becoming Superman, "Dumas Turn" *Concho River Review*, "Calling the Cattle" *Denton Poets Assembly Collection*, "Curling Fawns" Connotations Press, "Christmas" *Southwestern American Literature*, "Lake Frog Blues" *Blue Rock Review*, "Carpe Diem" *Blue Rock Review*, "The Jugular" Dress Codes Project, "The Summer Every Fence Came Down" *Poetry Society of Texas Journal*, "Valentines" *Langdon Review of the Arts*, "I Will Not Hide" *Redefining Beauty*, Dos Gatos Press.

Cover photo, "The Silver Eyed One," by Faizel Ismail, www.faizelismail.com
Author photo by Martha Shepp, www.marthashepp.com
Cover design courtesy of Nancy Parsons, www.graphicdesigngroup.net

Library of Congress Cataloging-in-Publication Data

Names: Morton, Karla K., author.
Title: Wooden lions / Karla K. Morton.
Description: First edition. | Huntsville, Texas : Texas Review Press, [2017]
Identifiers: LCCN 2017000901 (print) | LCCN 2017004756 (ebook) | ISBN 9781680031256 (pbk. : alk. paper) | ISBN 9781680031263 (ebook)
Subjects: LCSH: Animals--Poetry.
Classification: LCC PS3613.O77864 A6 2017 (print) | LCC PS3613.O77864 (ebook) | DDC 811/.6--dc23
LC record available at https://lccn.loc.gov/2017000901

This book is dedicated to all my companions who have walked with me along this Good Red Road:

Major, Smokey, Tucker Turtle, Pepe LePew, Kegler Von Bonner, Creampuff, Rusty, Eunice, Buck, Reveille, Misty, Pepper, Micho, Big Boy, Snickers, Frosty, Record, Butterfinger, Jet, KoKo, Pinot Noir, and Pontus, and to all those I've yet to know.

These are the souls who have saved me.

Contents:

Wooden Lions

Innocents and Fools

It struck me today
that I am older
than my father ever was.

Actually, the day I turned 27,
I passed him,
his last thoughts of my mother,
and myself—7 months and ready,
rushing to pick us up.

Looking in the mirror, I wonder
what part of my face is his,
I, who have been blessed a thousand fold,
taken in at two
by another father.

Mom told me she passed a field
the other day,
three tiny puppies huddled
by the gate, abandoned,

when, miraculously,
a police car appeared
coming down the road.

She flagged him down,
watched him gather them,
scared and shivering.

It is said God takes care
of innocents and fools.
How often I have wondered
which one I am.

Post War Amendments

After reading how the Nazi's
charged one-way tickets
to the concentration camps,
(half price for children)
then shot their pets before their eyes
as they boarded the trains,

I immediately stood,
and found the spider I smashed
still in the window—
picked up his body
of tiny crumpled sticks,
and took him outside and buried him;

worried how easy it becomes
to crush the innocent;
wondering if it might be time
to add a cruelty clause
to humanity's list of commandments,

starting with Revelations:
Hurt not the earth, neither the sea, nor the trees;
smash not unsuspecting spiders,
nor shoot cats, bunnies or dogs;
and never, never, never
gas the little children.

Of Night and Flesh

A long day of funeral arrangements,
I come back and build a fire,
and the snow begins—full fat flakes.

Stirring the logs, I think about this night,
his body turning back to ash,
remembering a story I heard years ago—

how the coyotes gather and bed down
on the south side of the crematorium
on frigid nights;
the heat of that great furnace
moving through steel and plaster
and mortar and brick,
warming the outside of the building.

He never liked the cold,
so we will wait until Spring,
and take his ashes and cast them into
his favourite place—the Sangre de Cristos.

Once you give yourself to the mountain,
you can never go back.

I think about the red coals of the fire—
so much better than the cold Earth;
I think about the smile on his face as he died.
I think about wild coyotes curled against warm brick;
his body turning to flame.

Bark Love, Bark

—with special thanks to Operation Kindness in Carrollton, Texas

This dog,
    let me tell you,
This dog
    is not afraid of *anything*.
This dog,
    who comforts me
in the roughest storms,
    who doesn't mind
    the thunder, the lightning

    is only bothered by a bath—
    beaten in his early life
before the pound

    by some cruel man
    in a hat
    with a garden hose.

Come here baby,
this is not the way life is done.

You who bark
    at men in hats;
who runs
    tail down from the hose,

this is why you have come to *me*
and my silly ways
to lay at my feet,
and sleep in my bed.

Bark Love, Bark
    at anyone who *ever* makes you feel him
    all over again.

Persephone, the Bear

A 911 call about a bear in a kitchen,
and the firemen dispatched,
setting a trap with peanut butter . . .
and there she was.

It was the closest I'd ever been
to a bear—her gentle brown eyes
and triangle head;
her massive claws.

A summer of drought and fires
brought her down,
this goddess of Spring,
lured by hummingbird feeders

and dog food,
and a bowl of pomegranates
on the other side
of that cabin door.

It was protocol—
a trespassing bear was caught,
tranquilized and tagged,
then taken out to the wilderness

and inflicted with fear—
what the firemen dreaded—
yelling, throwing sand bags,
branches, stones,

firing shotguns; revving chainsaws;
then releasing trained bear dogs
to chase her back,
up into the mountain,

hopefully to never return;
knowing if they failed,
and *Brown Bear 377*
with the yellow ear tag

was caught again,
she would be killed . . .
the blood still fresh in the cage
from the last captive.

Ah, let the angels comfort her,
help her to forget the crunchy,
the salt and the sweet
of the underworld;

let her live to tell great grand-bears
about the cruel devils down there;
their lusty, forbidden foods;
those horrible, hellish hounds.

If James Dean Could Fly

"Teenagers scare the living shit out of me."
—My Chemical Romance

They seem to walk more with their heads
than those four-toed claws;
legs, long and gangly;

shooed away and shot at
during loud parties
along strip malls and intersections.

Grackle . . . even the name is sharp; awkward.

One struts my way,
his one good eye
cocked towards me in pity—

my flat face and missing wings;
my two planks of feet,
big and earthbound;

this gothic teenager,
feathers turned up at his neck,
his coat so black, it's blue.

Trout Zen

Seven days at this cabin pass like one,
the song of the fish
the only music
I need. Chipmunks and deer, hooked on crackers,
come around about dusk; Christmas coloured

hummingbirds the size of my fist, diving
loudly overhead.
My first summer here,
I left out sugar-water for them, but
summoned the bears to the front door, tossing
furniture in the night, laughing at this
mountain amateur.

Trout hide in these waters, along edges
stilled by logs and brush;
cold bellies skimming
mossy rocks, wanting nothing more than slow,
fat flies; lullabies of rushing waters.

End of the World

> *Ancora Imparo*   (*I am still learning*)
> —Michelangelo, on his 83th birthday

Today, at 6 p.m., when the world
was predicted to end, I came upon
four geese and eleven goslings
in the shaded grass by the lake,

and realized, I've never *seen*
baby geese, just adults,
resting in local ponds,
or in a skein across the sky,

honking voices traveling for miles . . .
But I've never seen a gosling—
yellow grey, with no feathers,
glorious sheens of down

I wanted to touch, but momma
rushed up, tall as my thighs,
opened her pink mouth,
and in her quiet ferocity,

hissed until I scooted back.
And if today *is* the day we all die,
how perfect to spend my last hours
with these graceful prophets of the seasons;

learning this day—perhaps the last day
of my life, a *sound*; a sacred sound
while down on my knees,
eye to eye with mother goose;

a whisper as intimate as a thickening
of quills; the turning of a page;
a hungry Summer suckling
the tender breast of Spring.

May 21, 2011

In Defense of Regionalism

This is not a poem about cattle,
sprinkled like huge black beans
around a windmill;

or the pale blue compass sky—
clouds in each direction;

or Easter in New York,
when each tree finds the strength
to blush purple
in their tiny slant of sun;

or the million heads of corn
keeping watch over my firstborn
in Indiana.

It's about those two syllable
words of joy
the red bird sings
in the heat of the day,

after she finds the little glass bowl of water
on the porch;
her black beak
still wet.

Lost Cat

She showed up dry on the back porch
Not even one raindrop on her fur

She must have been close by
She must have heard me out walking

in the vicious storm, calling
calling her name for hours

my voice blurred in her dark hideaway
by rattling windows and bouncing hail

And here she is, as if this were any
other night, sitting calmly by the door

heeding the voice pummeling the earth
and shaking the trees, instead of this simple human's

My call, cracking like crooked lightning
Her answering thunder, a thousand miles away

Prayers for Cats

I don't know why they come to my house to die,
but they do

behind flat top bushes, curled up next to cool
bricks, a paw

over their faces. Maybe they had been here
before, for

a taste of dry cat food, watching me sing to
the roses

or lay my ear on the oak trees, listening
to the thrum

of old cello hearts . . . or maybe they just watched
in silence

from the shadows, as cats do, as I buried
their brothers,

triangle ears ticking forward to my prayers,
each Amen

punctuated with a rock upon their grave.

The One Who Loves Me

I do not tell her my heart crumbles
as she struggles to the sofa,
or when I feel her frail bones
beneath her fur.

Yet, every night she comes to me,
curling up on my pillow,
and I tell her she is beautiful,
and thank God for this soul

who fills my darkness;
who purrs me back to sleep
each time I stir;
this whiskered angel

who has loved me so well.

Summer of the Pig

One morning they appeared—
nine tiny pink bodies,
curling ribbons of tail,

hungry from the start;
the soft grunts and flat snouts
rooting for teats
on the belly of that old tired sow.

Quick minded,
in three days they learned *to sit,*
to stay, to come,
as I leveled troughs
sweetened with scraped scraps from our plates.

And I, the young shepherd of these squealing pink shoats,
following my voice like lambs.

Void of sweat glands,
they reveled in their daily bucket baths—
holding still and smiling as I rubbed red clay
off their coarse coconut bodies,
and wrapped them in frayed patterned towels,

losing two to suffocation
beneath the sow refusing to get up,
though I hollered, shoved;
viced her tail with pliers.

They were mine all summer,
and we sang and squealed and hiked
those 20 acres, staff in hand
for three months,
30 legs;
7 snouts;
one nose,

till September and school,
when they grew into sows and hogs,
turning triad ears down
to the ancient whispers of the earth,

with no memory of my voice
when I returned
and called each by name.

The Summer of the Pig
plowed under like the dried stalks
of sweet corn,
and bare rooted clay.

Then came the winter,
and a freezer full of pork,
white paper pounds
of bacon and tenderloin,

Sunday night treats
of sausage wrapped in pancakes;

when I walked the flats without song,
the tap of my staff keeping time,
the old tired sow
alone and pregnant
in her pen.

Port Aransas, 2061

History is best left to historians—
the *who* and the *what* and the *when*
of the world since 2011.
Philosophers will tell you the *why.*

A child born at this stroke of my pen
will have *already* lived half his life
by the time this poem is lifted to the sun
and read . . .

But let me tell you about the Chimney Sweeps
passing up from Peru;
how they search for safe roosts on their journey;
hanging five deep from the bricks;

how, in the mornings as they leave,
a few fall to the ground, their short lives over,
the weight of their bodies held by the others
until it is time to move on.

Port Aransas called to us since the moment
we stood upon her dunes and smelled her—
that womanly musk of heat and salt;
and we gather here again; honouring

those before us, and after—
the tiny beings that we are,
huddled together
in this jeweled chaos of wind and sea;

each as welcome as sand across our threshold;
holding quick to one another;
hearts great with direction and dreams,
no bigger than a bird in the hand.

—*Buried in the Port Aransas, Texas Time Capsule*

Something to Believe In

There was a moment today
as the sun was drifting down a sky
soft and thick and orange,
when a V of geese flew by;

and I smiled,
filled with something that reached
into my heart, like a breeze
through tiny wind chimes.

There are times I cannot name the magic
that comes humming through my soul,
but I know the geese felt it—

the glad madness of their song;
the last bits of light
clinging beneath their wings.

Mosquitoes

Sluggish, their bellies full,
I slapped them dead
against my leg, my own blood splayed
like red polish on my thigh.
Sure, they hover *now*,
but where were they years ago,
my body full of chemo,
and me out, sleeveless
in the Texas dusk, daring them
to take *just one bite?*
I didn't want their pity;
waiting; watching
as they would light upon my arm,
then fly on; bodies hungering;
piercing everyone but me.

The Golden. The Round.

—for Cheryl Toh

There is an artist I know
who creates in the night—
abstract paintings surfacing every dawn,
with found objects, papers, wax,
silks thin as hummingbird wings.

And in her work are circles—
hundreds of circles
linked like chainmail;

and I suddenly recalled a legend of Vietnam
about a giant, golden turtle in a lake
in the Thanh Hóa Province
that appeared with a sword
that helped win the battle against
Chinese invaders in the 16ᵗʰ Century.

The turtle rose once more, afterwards,
to reclaim the sword from the Emperor.

And recently, a turtle weighing
400 pounds was found
in the Hoàn Kiếm Lake—
a rare turtle with a soft, golden shell
called Rafetus swinhoei—
believed to be the last one of its species;
found in the *exact* same lake as the legend.

There are certain times in our lives
when we are given a glimpse
into the sacred—
answers that bring some kind of order to this world,
that make us believe in miracles,
in beauty;

abstract circles binding the past to the present;
a knowing . . . as if some foreign language
has been translated in our hearts;
as if some delicate strength has made us whole.

Finches

—for my parents, Pete and Wanda Martin

I went home today,
sitting outside with Mom and Dad,
the early March sun
warming the back of our heads
in the cool winds,

and talked about finches.
Not war, or Libya, or taxes;
or the price of gasoline;
or Alzheimer's;

but *finches*,
how those unassuming grey bodies
flit from feeder to limb;
their tiny yellow breasts
exploding *gloriously* into song.

The Glorious Black

If I were a vulture,
I would sit on the highest tower,
and I would turn my face
to the wind, letting it smooth
my bare head
and glorious black feathers;
and I would gaze over the mesquites
of Laredo, and smile.

If I were a vulture,
I would yearn for that moment
when I step off the tower
and begin to fall,
spreading my 6-foot wings—
my glorious black wings,
to ride that current of air.

If I were a vulture,
my song would be the wind—
that tiny swoop of sound
beneath each quill
as I spiral down to the feast
on the side of the road.

And I would eat the speed
of the rabbit;
the cunning of the coyote;
the stamina of the bull;
the tenderness of the deer.

And I would fly back up
to the highest perch
to watch that great light descend,
stretch my wings,
and merge with the darkness—
that black ripe darkness
disappearing between each star.

Weatherford Cougars

He never knew his grandfather,
who died years before he was born
from a reported suicide—
shooting himself twice,
then setting himself on fire.

Years later, his grandmother
married her son's best friend—
a carpenter and stone mason
who built her a fine house,
with a gun rack right over the door,

and two large bay windows.
She liked watching him come and go,
knowing wide horizons hold no secrets;
always on the lookout
for the big circling cats.

Building the Ark

Tossing the last log on the fire,
I won't let this night go—
five days on the river,
and I am reborn.

I walk the insulated concrete forms
of our cabin; the skeleton
of a place, *our* place,
rising up from the dirt;

a place to sleep in mountain air;
a place to long for, miles away
in the city.
In weeks, walls will be up—

bones of trees turned sacred
with a piercing of nails.
But now, I walk the perimeter,
a new constellation under

Red River stars.
Two by two, deer leap in
and out of our bedroom; our porch;
raccoons scuttle dirt floors,

all of them blessing what's to come:
long nights in white sheets;
showers of winter moons
through fresh, polished glass.

Clowns and Dark Water

She said there were certain things
in this world
she just couldn't handle—
made up things, like fantasy,
or science fiction.

Unicorns were at the top of her list.

I nodded, understanding,
thinking about my own fears,
just as odd, I suppose—
fears from the underbelly of reality:

snarling lips beneath painted on smiles;
dark currents of lurking creatures
with eyes that never close.

Lake Spiders

They are Hairy or Crunchy,
black and bushy with white dots and fangs;
or taut, water balloon bodies
with thin, tarsal claws tapping like pin tips;

arriving instantly—the first day of boating,
claiming every corner in the night;
webs heavy in rolled bugs each morning,
and I, goliath in their many eyes,

shrieking as Hairy emerges—
the size of a walnut—
more mammal than arachnid,
too big to swat;

trying to scoot him overboard,
but he refuses retreat,
having braved the arena,
the crowd now frenzied.

Then, with raised shoe in hand,
my swing freezes as he lifts his face
to look at me—*right up at me*,
tiny eyes above iridescent green lobes.

I halted; *stunned* . . . and he charged,
second limbs straight like spears,
cornering me till I had no choice but to kill.
And I, strangely remorseful

on the death of this woolly gladiator;
though he could have easily taken *me*
as he advanced in those short, gliding thrusts—
his eight legs, never seeming to move.

A Young Life

On Fridays and Mondays,
the trout man comes
from the Red River Hatchery,
two huge nets full of wide eyes;
gasping gills.

I love to watch their surprise
as they are freed into the cold rush;
the way they are stunned for a moment
before darting off to explore
every crevice and hidden root.

But sometimes, one doesn't make it,
its delicate white belly slowly turning up,
its body left to the whims of current.

It is hard to explain such a young loss—
those little souls not made
for the wild river,
the treacherous falls,
the piercing hooks of man.

Those We Meet Along the Journey

I dreamt last night I met a woman,
and was frightened by her smile—

her teeth like the tiny sharp hairs
of the starfish I found on the beach—

still soft and pliable, body ripped in half
on its journey from the ocean floor.

How many times, I wonder, have we *all*
come across such outcasts;

fearful of pierce and sting;
contemplating the mysteries

of where they've been;
the darkness, the heartaches,

the rough waves of Fate
on the way to each shore.

Helplessness

The first thing I thought of was the Holocaust Museum—
huge glass boxes full of shoes—empty shells of men,

women, children, infants, all tossed together; shed
right before they stepped, naked, into gas chambers.

My mind leaped to an IMAX film I had seen, about
African elephants that found exposed bones of kin,

beasts that had died in the endless drought. They stopped,
rubbed their trunks along the ribs and femurs and tusks,

and mourned . . . a cry . . . a *wail* I can't seem to forget.
Standing in a parking lot in Laredo, knee-deep in a pile

of bleached animal skulls . . . I was back in that place *again*—
that place of total human helplessness;

that circle of anger and horror; a sickness in my gut, like pain;
my mind trying to process such cruelty—

If *only* those bones could've been put to rest in God's earth;
if *only* those shoes could've been worn thin by play.

May Day

He had been a baby;
a tiny little baby;
innocent; swaddled.

It is said his mother
even contemplated abortion,
but her doctor talked her out of it.

He had been a toddler,
on his knees on the floor,
laughing, twirling, playing.

How do we mark the turns in a life?
When does a child
morph into monster?

May Day has a new celebration
to add to Mozart's Figaro, the polio vaccine,
the announcement of Hitler's demise—

the death of Osama Bin Laden,
shot over the left eye,
chum at the bottom of the ocean.

May 1st. Let us celebrate all things Spring—
the beauty, the healing, the cleansing;
flowers in our hair.

I cannot mourn the monsters of this world,
just those little boys—crumbs on their shirts,
wooden lions in their hands,

boys who, one day,
fell into the well of darkness,
and never, *never* came back.

The Lion. The Lioness

Come to me.
Come to me like the river's roar,
like ravens at the morning's door.

There's no knock;
no bronzed lion to pound and wake,
just yawning dawns; the lush daybreaks

opening
like sunrise. I, your troubadour
will sing across your kitchen floor;

enough warmth
to stay the dark; to overtake
each fear, each tear the wicked make

slip your cheeks.
Let my arms be your sacred shore;
may loneness haunt you nevermore.

I, the flawed,
give you my sovereign heart to take—
each bounty, glory, each mistake

forgiven;
clasping hands through destiny's door.
Let us be fearless. Let us roar.

Pontus

He found me at the pound,
quiet werewolf eyes calling louder
than all the yapping around us.

It was three months before he barked,
the intensity startling us both—
waiting for my laughter before wagging,

and at my side ever since,
asking only for rolled down windows;
sleeping at my feet.

My great-grandmother told me she felt it her fault
my father died so young—said he was her favourite
grandson—that she loved him too much.

But I don't believe in *too much*.
I don't believe in a God who trades heart for brimstone.
And I *love*—
I love as though my body would burst into flame—

my man, my children, my moon, my river,
even a dog who will crush my foolish heart,
leaping seven years ahead each birthday.

But now, see him lope the snow
and chase the deer;
youth springing his long legs;
his tail always laughing.

And oh, let us love one another;
let us turn our souls inside out—
God in the seams, the loose stitches;
the shaggy head beneath our hand.

Singing Doves

whetted my need for you, with their fevered
calls; their dance from fence to bush to hidden

nest; music, like ours, with gasps and tiny
chords, small noises as we move across sheets,
never still; movements of lips and fingers

and wrapping thighs; clutching bodies . . . Outside,
winds stir heated feathers; cricket legs bend

like harp strings.

Elk Tango

It was late
on that winding road
when I first
saw his face—
that magnificent creature,
mighty; unstartled.

Enchanted,
I was drawn to his
animal
charisma;
and had I four legs, followed
him into the woods.

And I knew,
in that one moment,
survival
in the wilds
or in this life, took a trust
between the genders,

a trust that
man was strong enough
to lead and
to protect;
that woman was strong enough
to choose to follow.

Human Goodness

I don't know how-
the palm trees opened up my greedy heart.
Adam Zagajewski

Who, among us has not coveted the sea,
the peace of the water,
escaping the ugliness of people
who crush the tiny shells of our spirit.

We, who all have our demons—
the tentacles,
the poison tips,
the black ink of each soul.

But days of palm and sand
have taught me this:

the tide comes
the tide goes;

creatures become stranded
feet from salvation;

and out of the hundreds
who stomp our shadows
every day,

there is always one
who will stop,
and see the need,

and find the hard quill
of fallen feather,
and gently roll us
back into the sea.

Noble Skunk

Dad brought him home
in a cardboard box;
this tuft of black hair—
two white stripes down the back;
stink box surgically removed;
saved from an empty apartment.

A new cage came next,
three feet long; four feet off the ground—
a new home and cartoon name:
Pepe LePew.

He took to me and I became his caregiver,
rushing home each day to try to tame him
with dog food and carrots,
but all he wanted was *down*—
onyx claws squirming for earth.

Months later, he bit my mother;
an ancient eye-tooth
through fingernail and bone,
and we finally understood

this beast of no apology;
this beast born for the moon and the wild
and the curl of damp holes.

And we drove him out to the forest,
opened the steel doors,
and watched him reclaim his name
as he raced to the trees—

Noble Skunk;
bushed tail high in the air;
those twilight eyes
never once looking back.

Cattlemen's Epiphany

On special occasions, we'd go on Friday nights,
fresh polish on Dad's shoes;
Mom's diamond heart, sparking at her neck
from the red table candles;
scooting heavy barrel chairs out, then in;
a red napkin in each lap.

There, in that dark room,
I learned which fork for the salad,
how to order a meal and cocktail—
Roy Rogers, exotic with cherries,
how to anchor the knife on the plate,

and it was there, surrounded by huge photos
of *Queen Manso II of LSU; Domestic Mischief,
Miss Zato, Lady Rex,* and *Prince of Red Gate,*
when I realized *those* were the beasts
I was eating—the filet on my plate.

Stunned, I compared those Champions—
their well-brushed hides, thick loins
and peaceful eyes, with the glorious sizzle
of steak, and . . . as though it were my first . . .
took a bite; welcoming those bravado bodies

into mine; savouring; swallowing
the wild power of the bull; the grass he ate;
the sun inside the grass, even the mud,
and ached for the night—
when I could fall upon my knees,
eyes tight with prayer; anxious to tell God
I *finally* get it—
the sacrifice; the body; the blood.

—*Cattleman's Steakhouse, Ft. Worth Texas*

Do You Hear What I Hear?

Our first Christmas in North Carolina,
we found ourselves stranded;
three feet of snow and ice,
our propane tank drained
from stupidity—

the electricity clicking off
in a great down-swerve of sound—
taking out the heat of our argument
with the lights, and dishwasher
and washing machine,
and Christmas CD's;

our marriage teetering
like the stacked stone walls
around the yard—
balancing only by gravity
and the lack of hard blows,

when we heard a whimper—
opening the door
to a Doberman puppy,
bringing him in from the storm;

swaddling him in blankets
next to the meager fire;
a tiny soul we both could reach for;
his tail as long as a kite.

Dove at my Door

For two days the grey dove has been at my door
Singing his sweet song of longing
It's you love I'm sure, it wasn't there before
Each day as the sun is dawning

He comforts me with his sweet song of longing
Protecting my heart from the frost
Each day he's here as the soft sun is dawning
Think of all we had, and not lost

You protected my heart from winter's scowl frost
Warming our nest-bed together
I must think of, now, all we had, and not lost
Souls like ours are trussed forever

And now you've flown from our nest-bed together
Farewells—there was no time before
But the grey dove sings of love that's forever
Two days now, he's been at my door

Mountain Melon Thieves

Ah, that we were *all* so lucky—
to have to lock the house at night,
not in fear of some violent stranger,
but Momma Bear,

her two cubs in tow,
who smells the cantaloupe
we sliced for supper;

who knows we always leave the skins
in the black little bin

on the other side of that thin-paneled door.

Semi-Stalkers

Often snakes come into my dreams
like they do my home—
glamorous party guests
whom *everyone* knows,

leaving their thin chiffon scarves
as gifts
on the kitchen floor
or doorstep.

Though I've moved eleven times,
they've always found me,
somehow charming
the post-mistress for my address.

Tucked between concrete
at Pecan and 1st,
I smile.

Perhaps this time I've shaken them,
like Tom—
Vietnam sharpshooter
turned policeman
turned milkman.

Often he'd let himself in my locked doors,
this morning visitor—
done with work by 10 am,
beer in hand,
Looney Tunes turned down low,
my refrigerator stocked with chocolate milk.

Sometimes I wake in the middle of the night
and think about these gifts
and pray:
Let me not be ungrateful.
Let the Winchester always be oiled.

Dinner and a Show

Growing up, I savoured those
last pink minutes of dusk
before the sun went down;

before the rush and worry of time,
which bolted on with the streetlights.
Then time to be home, to wash up,

set the table, do the dishes, bag
the trash, take a bath, get to bed.
Today, not much has changed—

I leave the house lights off
to watch the sun crayola the walls,
and darken the redbirds.

Soon, hungry teens
and a suit-heavy husband
will clamour in, whisking the house

in a bowl of fluorescent bulbs;
daily drama; rising decibels
of speakers. Possums gather

at the windows, laughing at the
flurry; chomping fistfuls of June bugs,
like brown, popped corn.

Leaving Loose the Reigns

—for my daughter, Kathryn

She has a sense about her—
a magic the young possess;
a knowing brought with them
through the womb;
a trust that rain will fall
when they thirst;
wheat will bloom when they hunger.

Balking at the jeep or 4-wheeler,
she prefers the horse
on these steep mountain trails
wrenched with switchbacks
and unsurviveable cliffs;
leaving loose the reigns,

believing in a beast that can
smell the hidden holes
of burrowed creatures.
My legs clench around my mare
as I watch her on her horse,
inches from a chasm;
fearless . . .
a life more precious than the stars.

Ghost Letters

One hundred years ago,
it took the Pony Express
three to five days
to deliver mail from one end
of the States to another.
Today, in our highly advanced,
technology-modernized post offices,
the average delivery time
of a letter sent across the country is . . .
well . . . five to ten days.

Of course, there are faster methods—
day curriers or overnight flights,
but the basis of our postal system
seems not to be so much about the time,
but about trust—
knowing the stamp or the horse
or the jeep with the wrong-sided wheel
will take the mail safely where it needs to be.

It's like my dear friend, a Scotsman,
who always sends his kilt to the US
by mail . . . saying it's the essence
of his history, his family, his blood . . .
much too valuable to trust with the airlines.

And my brother, in the Air Force,
who never trusts movers to ship
his irreplaceable photo albums and medals
from station to station.
He always posts them first by mail.

I went to your house, and packed up
all those treasures you loved so dearly,
and brought them safely to my home . . .
and you followed.

For weeks I have heard you—
the upstairs television comes on;
a cool breeze finds me
when the windows are closed;
toilets spontaneously overflow,
the broken kitchen clock
suddenly began keeping perfect time.

You died so quickly, so unexpectedly.
You didn't have time to secure your precious things,
to make sure everything was taken care of.
But yesterday, I came upstairs when you called—
the squeaky bedroom door slightly moving back and forth.
And I walked up there, into the room that holds your things,
and I went through them all,
and found your jewelry,
which I sent to your daughter and granddaughters;
the bronze Remington's I delivered to your grandsons;
the statue of Alexander to your daughter;
and the 20 dollar gold piece that your grandfather gave you,
was mailed safely home to your son.

The time has come now, for *you* to move on;
time to reach *your* final destination.
I don't know eternity's address,
so I'll mark an envelope HEAVEN
and put extra stamps on it,
and drop it into the gentle flames of the fire,
trusting you can reach out to a wisp of rising smoke
and it will curl around your airy fingers,
and lead you up to Pegasus
who waits in the dark, and the wind,
and the snow, and the sleet, and the hail
to carry you
up, where you finally need to be.

Texas Longhorns

I always thought them the loneliest of creatures—
perfectly happy to be on their own for days at a time,
and when they *are* together,
they are unable to breech that deadly horn-span
that keeps them apart.

No side by side touching,
no hugs.
Self-sufficient and tough;
smart and gentle.

My father and brother sit at the supper table,
heads down, eating,
four feet of silence between them.
Women come and go and hover and peck
like cow birds,
but *they* need nothing more
than food when they hunger,
the sun on their backs,
and miles of barbed wire to mark what's their own.

When Man and Deer Combine

—for Ray Drone

There is a man down in San Angelo
who tracks the white-tailed deer;
who follows their thin, winding trails
through the thickets and by the rivers
and into the mountains,
collecting shed antlers.

And he takes them home,
and holds them, and studies them;
then carves out the most beautiful writing pens
you've ever seen.

When I first saw them, I couldn't resist
their warm cream and brindle colours.
When I first held them,
their tender curves and weight
seemed to balance perfectly
in the nest of my fingertips.
I *had* to own one; *had* to bring it home.

To hold such art, such beauty,
such *gentle wildness* in your hands,
simply moved me to tears.

But when I haphazardly tucked it
into the twists of my hair,
it held fast to the gathered bun,
as if that's what it was meant to do;
as if it had been born again on another creature
—regal and wild—
proudly bursting forth
from the bundled crown atop my head.

Season of the Widow

I've always heard
everything has its season,
even the birds, like the scissortails.

Certain tribes consider them sacred
from of their simultaneous flight—
flight in their wings, of course, but also in their tails.
It's as though they're *human*,
with a double journey in life—
one in the body, the other in the soul.

But one year seemed different.
There were *multitudes* of black widow spiders,
when it had been so long since I'd seen even *one*.

Perhaps there are those times in our lives,
like that year—full of death, void of any seasons
except survival,
when the black widows abound;
when winter hasn't the energy to freeze;
when tomatoes grow thick and soggy and rotten;
when sunflowers hang peakish towards the ground;
and stoic scissortails
sit untraveled on the wires.

When each night, the stars hide,
and the only constellations to be seen
are two red triangles, tip to tip
on the bellies of all those shiny black arachnids—
seemingly the *only* things on this earth
alive and bright and busy,
building straight-line webs,
waiting, crouched and ready
in the corners.

Aye, indeed, there *is* a season of survival,
when all we can do
is drag our heads off the pillow,
lift tasteless toast to our mouths,
and get through the grey of each day
armed only with the pointed toe of a shoe.

Save the Camels

It was a wise man who first noted
how much a piece of hay weighs—
a piece so light, you could easily
blow it out of your hand
with a simple puff of breath,
like a feather.
And who could ever imagine
that a ton of feathers
weighs the same as
a ton of iron chains?
That wise man could.
And I bet he also knew
the weight of words—
a seemingly harmless bunch of alphabet
thrown together—but when uttered,
take flight into the universe
like a floating feather,
or a piece of hay
that feeds the heifers,
brains the scarecrows,
swaddles babes in a manger.

But the cruel ones
seem to be a little heavier,
taking aim when they're released—
landing hard and piling up
on the rough humped backs
of all those poor, unsuspecting camels.

The Perfect Gentleman

"Nothing will ever sting you,
if you just hold your breath"
—Loyd Counts

The wasp landed in my elbow,
his weapon, curled and tucked

in front of him as though
he were holding his top hat in

his hands—my breathlessness,
his gold-foiled invitation. He

must have seen how gently you kissed
that very spot; must feel

the faint dew of your tongue.

Summer Solstice

This is the day of new beginnings;
earth turning her face to the sun;
pacing bees, anxious for flowers
to open their watery eyes,
tears thick with nectar.

It's the day of the longest light,
when we sit by the creek,
waters cool from dark springs
tumbling over our calves, our toes,
whisking the heavy heat from our skin.

It's the day of coming forth—
the wedding of heaven and earth,
pollens floating like tossed rice,
dragonflies dancing in the aisles,
morning willed from night.

And somewhere in the leafy green,
a bird opens her beak,
and from the tiny darkness
of her throat,
a song.

The Dumas Turn

A road trip out, I missed the Dumas turn,
and crossed the blessed border; crossed the Red;
and armed with maps, and hours of sun to burn,
I took an old, forsaken road instead.

White prairie primrose grew in long pale beds,
and beasts, like Vegas showgirls, trim and firm,
would lift, in perfect rhythm, kicking legs;
a road trip out, I missed the Dumas turn.

Astounded now, my kids began to squirm,
for they had never *known* my truck to tread
off *any* highway—they had never *learned*
to cross the blessed border; cross the Red.

And when those antelope flew, we were fed
with beauty that leaped out in every turn.
I vowed to teach them both, too city-bred,
with just a map, and hours of sun to burn.

I taught them *magic*—how to look, and yearn
and churned caliche dust that wisped and fled
beyond the dirt path, past that Dumas turn,
and took an old, forsaken road instead.

Calling the Cattle

We humans have a love of cattle—
with bodies thick and bells that rattle;
with skinny tails made just for whipping;
and busy mouths all wet and dripping;
and furry ears that keep on thinking
they're hearing windmills spin for drinking.

But one time when they needed drinking,
their ears were pricked—such thirsty cattle.
They heard a sound that got them thinking—
a long snort-snort; a little rattle—
could this be some cool water dripping?
They looked around through winds a whipping,

and followed close those sounds a whipping—
could these sounds lead to cattle drinking?
And then they ran, their wide mouths dripping,
Angus, Longhorns, all breeds of cattle
who came because of all this rattle,
water was calling, they were thinking . . .

But it *wasn't* what they were thinking,
and yes, they heard some winds a whipping,
but what, they found, in this great rattle,
was not just water for their drinking,
and in surprise to all the cattle,
was just a human, wet and dripping!

And in a tub! Her long toes dripping!
But she was sleeping, and not thinking
about her sounds, which called the cattle,
who raced to find *no* windmill whipping,
and more than water just for drinking,
but *snoring*, what a vicious rattle!

And oh, how loud! Those doors did rattle!
Her long toes kept the water dripping.
But those great bovines wanted *drinking*,
and put their boney heads to thinking
how they could move that girl by whipping
their tails—oh, mischievous cattle!

Rattle woke her *RUN!* she was thinking
and jumped out, dripping; wet hair whipping,
and left her tub for cattle, drinking.

Curling Fawns

nestled in the sun
against the riverbank.
I curled into winter-dead grasses
and withered leaves
next to the river—*my* river—
faithful muses pouring over rocks
and fallen limbs;
suddenly unafraid of spiders,
or time,
or the cold shoulder of night;
the weight of my body
flattening the brush
like the fawn I startled this morning—
her round pocket of earth,
still warm.

Le Poisson

Every year, I watch him grow long and thick,
in waters pooled by roots and captured brush,
holding my breath as fishermen in slick
waders, lure with intricate flies; shiny
hooks; smiling as they curse and stomp away—
shaking their heads, slapping poles in a spray
of water. And every morning, coffee
in hand, I cast my face in his tiny
lagoon, searching for his quivering fins,
wondering if he knows I look for him.
Yet, for all my worry, I cannot save
him—this cold creature of the underworld;
this beast of silence and shadow and mud.

88: *Sign of the Cat*

—for Marsha Dowler

In the depression,
those out of work and destitute
had to stop at houses
along their paths
to humbly ask for drink or food,

leaving marks on the fences or doors
of the homes they'd been to—
secret messages for the others
following behind.

The drawing of a cat, 88, meant
A kind woman lives here.

So often these days,
it's the cats themselves in need—
the wild, the feral—
always seeming to find the homes
of kindhearted souls.

There must be a secret earmark
cats leave for one other
as they leap fences
and scurry the shrubs,

watching with silent, golden eyes
for the ones who fill the water
and clatter dry food;

some even braving forth
in thanks—
circling coils of 8's
around and around
our legs.

Feral Longhorn Angel

—Lost on Moccasin Trail, *Paisano Ranch, Austin, Texas*

I followed the path of coyote, raccoon and deer—
trusting the trail of droppings; of bones;
stepping over white rocks as curved and pocked
as broken skulls.

A shortcut it was, down from Farabee Lookout,
soon overgrown in Summer's best—
cedars, thorns, spider-fetched grasses;
but I trudged on, finally reaching the river.

The sun was low over the bluffs,
and I hurried to return on the trail
back to the road,
only to find the opposite riverbank.

So I turned, following pink plastic ribbons
tied high in cedars to mark the way,
ending up *again* at the river.
Back and forth; back and forth.
Ribbon to ribbon to ribbon.

Panic confusing my direction, the sun sinking,
I found the river again by the rope swing
I'd seen from the road,
deciding then to use the riverbed as my path.

Three moccasins later, I was forced back
into bank brush taller than my head,
an accordion of snakes at my feet;

a quick inventory:
half a canteen,
one dagger,
watch,
cell-phone, half battery left,

walking stick,
275 acres,

poisonous snakes,
wild roaming game,
dark in 30 minutes.

Terrified, I called out to God,
then waited . . .
but . . . Sun didn't stop its plummet,
moccasins didn't slither away,
spiders didn't burst into flame.

Sometimes the nature that must be changed
is our own.

And in the golden hour of my faith,
I charged forth, my walking stick, a rod
blessing each step;
head down, hat pushing through thicket and briar,
spiders gawking through balls of white web.

Thirty minutes I forged,
eventually emerging only ten feet from my truck,
falling to my knees in thanks,
hands sweating, clasped to my stick.

I do not know if I own the mettle
to protect such an Eden,
but this I learned—

a sacred coming-of-age happened out there
in the weeds and briars and snakes;

faith became something muscular and staunch:
a feral longhorn angel—two horns upon its head:

one, the voice that calls out;
the other, the silence that answers.

Christmas

There is nothing I could tell you to make you
believe—you either
do, or you don't. But there's magic here, around
us—whispered between

pale moths on moonless nights, when there's no work to
be done, no shaft of
moonlight to climb; their songs, filling their tiny
mouths, suspended in

the air, wafting down like dust on the pillows.
Intangible is
my love for you—beyond the round of your eyes;
your lips inside my

elbow. It's the way day sinks, blushing, sated
into night; the way
you've cupped my heart, mesmerized by strings of light,
wildly, silently,

fluttering within the dark warmth of your hands.

Lake Frog Blues

They must live the profession of patience—
anthropologists having to wait three years;
their prayers for drought
thudding upstream
against every other Texans'—

to shrink the waters
of Richland Chambers Reservoir
to find the bones of a black man, about 40,
perhaps a freed slave working that river bottom;
who started a grave yard
when they buried him where he fell.

A cemetery lost under years of rain—
washing away spent muscle; burned skin;
the blues and grays of war;
even his etched stones shuffled
somewhere downstream.

It's said ancient Rome
only believed in cremation;
didn't bury their people
until the coming of Christ;

never felt the need to contemplate
the afterlife;
never considered what old bones
could've told them from beneath
muddy waters—
why crawfish only *back*
into dark holes;
why lake frogs always sing
those same sad songs.

Inspired from a news story out of Navarro County
about a lost cemetery found in the drought under the lake.

Carpe Diem

I sat beside the river,
mesmerized by hundreds
of little flying bugs,
rising, hovering.

My brother said
they were like mayflies,
and *that's* where fly fishermen
like to be, knowing trout
can't resist their flutter;
their twirl.

Born on top of the water,
they rise up and mate,
then, before they die,
lay more floating eggs;
only living 24 hours.

And as day curtsied to night,
sunset spread her orange arms
upon the river,

and I caught my breath
as each bug rose
to their one, glorious day of life,
like tiny, golden gods.

Coyote Medicine

*It was Coyote that figured out how to steal fire from the gods
when Man was freezing, and has been our trickster teacher
ever since.* —Robert Oakes

Oblivious to nature,
they built a beautiful home,
decorating the front pond
with two expensive black swans -

plucking their wings
so they couldn't escape.
Weeks later, they woke,
horrified to find them devoured.

Coyote says *nothing* is sacred
and *everything* is sacred.
See how he scattered black feathers
on the edge of the pond;

knowing they would walk out
and stand beside water so still
they could not escape
their own reflection.

One Month to the Day After My Father Died

I found it in the bathtub, angered
someone left the cabin damper open.
And what was a bat to do
but seek out the downward chute
into that irresistible darkness?

Petite as a kitten,
she'd fit in my palm
with her delicate claws;
one fur covered wing
zigzagging to the side;

but as I tried to lift her,
she opened her wide pink mouth
and gave a gravelly hiss
that knocked me back;
miniature vampire teeth
against the shovel.

But I lifted her anyway,
and carried her outside,
and laid her beneath
some fallen branches;
this tiny warrior
who just wanted to be left alone;

I stayed for a while,
then . . . reluctantly . . . turned away;
cursing our helplessness;
our humanness;
that unknown darkness beyond our control.

Cow Trails

When the land began to roll,
I saw them on the top of the hill,
walking the horizon in a line,
like cattle like to do,
thick Angus bodies,
king against the blue.

And I wondered if they walked
this same path at night,
how their bodies would block the stars
in great cow silhouettes,
or, how in times of full moon,
the cool light would shine
on their black, glossy bodies.

And I, so happy on this same road
I've taken for years—the road leading
up to my mountains.

Perhaps, this
is the definition of happiness—
bovine lessons;
roads crossing left and right,
each one with its own adventures,

but I, content with my own trail;
my own boots,
a truck full of gas,
my dog curled in the back seat,
a walking stick, a bottle of whisky,
blending into the night;
following the stars, the moon;
the golden tail of setting sun.

The Summer Every Fence Came Down
(Barbed-Wire Reaction)

They ended up in the pasture next door—
the dark sway of the neighbour's
pure-bred Angus hips,
and her come-hither backward glance,
snapping the Longhorn's will power
like that old wooden fence . . .

And *all* the Longhorns followed.

And when their rancher came to fetch them,
Bossy spied his blue truck,
and began to . . . not jump . . . not buck—
but *leap* into the air, front hooves first,
arching in perfect bovine rainbows,
over and over again,
excited over the special truck,

the truck *she knew* carried
the sweet blocks,
the molasses sticks,
the cattle candy,
dancing in that caliche trail
as the others followed,
all the way back home.

And in the pasture to the east,
the bulls began to stir at the sight—
all that female bouncing;
all jowl and udder and horns.

The Bat Sequel

I was told I killed that bat
the moment I left her on the ground—
that bats can't rise and fly,
they must fall from a higher space
and glide first to fly.

I suppose that makes sense
in some odd kind of way.

Forgive me, Ms. Bat,
for serving you up
to the next famished beast
that passed.

Forgive my ignorant, human logic;
my silly, human arms.

The Jugular

You laughed when I said
I got out of the truck,
pocket knife in hand,
looking for the horse I just hit.

And what would you have done with that?

I would have wanted to end his suffering;
to cut his throat.

As if you ever could.

I hope I could have done it, if I needed to,
if he hadn't scampered off,
if he'd lain there, barely breathing in the ditch.

I hope I could wring a chicken's neck
if my children were hungry;
or wedge a rifle in the soft round ear
of a calf, half-mauled by coyotes;

or stand by your grandmother's bed,
like your grandfather did—
fighting the rest of the family's riot
for feeding tubes,
because *she did not want them.*

I'll admit, I've grown up soft,
my poultry comes plucked and quartered
from the grocery,
or fried up in the drive-through;
hot water flows at my touch.

But I can tell you, I like the sound my boots make
when they scuffle;

I pack a knife and compass and arrowhead
in my purse;

my phone holds the lunar calendar
and Morse-code apps;
there's a shovel under my back seat.

So, perhaps it's time to reconsider,
though I stand, 60 pounds less
beneath your chin.

Step back.
Take another look.
Size me up *again*
and decide
if I could find my way
to the jugular.

Copperhead

He'd show every summer
around the first week of high 90's,
body lounged against the back door,
stretched across the cool cement porch;

and I, safe with the thin screen door
between us, lying down,
pressing my finger against the holes
to feel his dry skin.

Not once did it seem to bother him—
No sudden curl of head or threat of fang.
And I would sing to him
those luscious summer months,

convinced he was lonely too—
that he knew me by my voice;
never fearful of leaf piles
or backyard campouts;

leading the way
on every forest adventure;
that same wordless tune
always on my lips.

A Day of Vegetarianism

My last night in Laredo, a clairvoyant
told me I would kill a creature on the road;
said I *had* to hit it, or my truck would roll;

I had to grip the steering wheel with both hands,
and power through. And I thought about myself,
one of seven billion people on this earth;

thought about all the animals I alone
had killed with fashion; with diet, with driving;
and vowed I would become, for just *one* day,

a vegetarian. I would take no life.
I caught a spider, and released it outside;
had tortillas and eggs for breakfast, veggie

soup for lunch; pasta for supper. And on my
way home, I drove slowly, held the wheel hard, kept
a careful eye on the edge of the forest.

Pleased with myself, I pulled into the drive, walked
to the house, and looked back at my truck—at the
tiny, brown sparrow embedded in the grill.

Enrapture

I heard the call of the leopard frog
deep in the January frost
after the coyotes yipped and slept
and the light of the stars was lost.

Trees stood still
Wind put down her comb
Night held her silvery breath
I listened to the call of the leopard frog
till only dark and need were left.

I heard the call of the leopard frog
and though I'm a child of the sun,
he calls for me from the throat of the earth—
I come, my love, I come.

Wishing On Sirius

How many have we buried?
How many times have we said, *never again?*
Yet, some things never change . . .

They show up in our lives, and we find ourselves
waiting for them to come in; *sleeping* head to head;
talking to them when there's no one around.

Old man Fry had one like that, back in the free-grass days,
when the sheep were plenty, and well-trained shepherd dogs
went for a hundred dollars.

He *loved* that dog—more than his hunting buddies;
more than music; more than any woman.
But he lost him once, not knowing his neighbour

up on Clear Creek had found him, and put him to work.
But one rainy night, Mr. Edleman didn't pilot him in,
and that dog took all 500 head of sheep, 14 miles to Denton,

and offered them up at Old Man Fry's front door—
Old Man Fry, who ran the meat market.
Who else could love us like that?

We walk, side by side, on this Good Red Road,
that same animal soul, searching us out each lifetime;
our one great companion in many forms.

I lean down to you, nose to nose;
rub your ears and your head, one more time.
You look up, give one slight of tail . . .

Days later, still grieving, I stare into the stars,
lost in this wide world without you.
I miss you, my friend.
Come . . . find me again.

—*History and Reminiscences of Denton County   by Ed. F.*
Bates pg. 399-400
—*Picture in the Courthouse Museum—97.17.22*
—*Sirius, the brightest star in the sky, is in the Canus Majoris,*
and appears in summer (thus the Dog Days of Summer).
Known as the Dog Star, or Orion's Dog, Sirius has been noted
by the Seri and Tohono O'odham tribes as the dog that follows
sheep.   The Cherokee considered Sirius as a dog-star guardian
of the "Path of Souls."

Black Mesa

It is a land of silence and secrets—
Rancho de San Juan,
named for the monk tortured
for his Queen's confessions,
but who took them deep into the earth.

Here, Ravens return each year
as black as their Mesa,
nesting in the sandstone,
and babies are born—

one falling to the ground,
the parents back and forth
with food and protection;
until the day

when *knowing*
seeps into his feathers
and he gleans his gift,
and rises.

This is the place of revelation;
the soul, emerging like blooms
through cactus teeth;

secrets of sand and scrub and saints
in rounded stone;
the ancient ways whispering in the wind;
our wings, hushed enough to hear.

—*Saint San Juan Nepmuceno*

Shiner

—for Donna and Ralph Willberg, Paint Rock, Texas

Never was there a dog
more fit for a man—
corralling the strays,
herding bleating bodies
into pens—

these goats,
dumb to everything
except her commands.

I bed next door,
where old John Deere
used to sleep,
oil stains tinting glossed concrete;

now a cottage with curtains;
antlers by the pairs
on walls, windowsills;

and think about all the dogs
who gift us each day
with their lives,
who instantly forgive
each cross word,

who grew old and limping
by our sides,
looking up at us as though
we were the gods.

Never have we felt so loved,
never slept so sound—
those triangle ears,
tuned and twitching
through the night.

Stag's Heart

—for George Alexander Louis, His Royal Highness Prince
George of Cambridge

Across the pond,
it unharbours the imagination—
this concept of Royalty;
of crowns and castles and Queens.

But I have been there,
seen the Changing of the Guard;
the horses, the hunt, the horn;
watched white-gloved hands
wave from long cars;

your history as deep and mystical
as the Woodlands;
a place of knights, bloodhounds
and swords;

And now, a new birth in the Kingdom—
a long-legged calfe emerges
from the ancient blue rivers.

Rise up, Little One,
drink the strength of your mother;
roar with the blood of your father.

My wish for you is that you see
your Grandmother's eyes in the mirror;
that your first steps are barefooted—
toes clenching earth as old as God Himself.

And in your quiet moments,
May the Red Deer of Wisdom
gently step from the forest—
that you may be humbled by the presence
of God given glory,
you, young Hart of the People.

Chrysalis

*—For Her Royal Highness Princess Charlotte Elizabeth Diana
of Cambridge*

Perhaps women know it best—
how heartbeat can burst from the blue;
from the damp grotto of womb.

We are of a goddess planet,
a world ruled by egg and moon
and butterfly.

Once, in great exasperation,
my eyes reached to the sky—
the place we go in need,
the realm of all blue beginnings,

and found *butterflies* . . .
thousands of monarch butterflies
in southbound migration,

my heart, releasing every question
for a moment of silent answers—

when beauty births forth
from its darkness;
into its own—
its auroral crown of light.

Valentines

The safest place I know waits across the river,
flanked by cedar and aspen sentries; the mountain
at its back. People ask about the kept woman

who feeds on silence, who caresses fallen leaves
like a lover, who spins mayflies into fairies,
who knows where trout hide. Snow rises up the windows,

curled bears slumber in dark tufts. I've heard the cuttle
of mountain lions at my door, delighted in
the bloody snow of some trespassing peeping tom.

Here, generations of deer know the sound of my
voice; the smell of saltines on my skin. Let the world
have its ways, I'll stay camouflaged in the thick arms

of the Forest—the one who keeps watch while I sleep.
And when I wake, ravens pull up the sun; heart-shaped
deer tracks, like valentines, lay scattered at my feet.

Laika

The first dog in space in 1957,
they built her capsule around her,
but made no provision for her return;
no rescue ever planned.

Somewhere above us
she still spins,
a paltry silver star
full of little doggie bones.

My dog Pontus has never flown,
but would gladly walk into a steel crate if I asked;
be rocketed into any universe I chose.

He would wag his tail
when I told him
All is well
and scratch his ears,
and give him rawhide.

He would trust in my return
even when hunger
surged
and devoured his flesh;

his eyes fixed
upon the screeching steel bolt
that never opened again.

My Old Cat

Down to 4 pounds,
her 13-year-old body
is sculpted
like the Red Rocks of Sedona.

There is no mistaking
the triptych head of the feline,
the arch of spine,
the long tail.

Used to, she'd only sleep with *me*,
balled against my décolleté,
her head in my palm;
her purr stirring each time I did.

But now, night calls her away,
her calico sliver of moon,
a tiny crescent
on the outside cushion,
or the mat by the stove;

her ears heeding a breath
greater than mine—
the stone sleep
of beloved old bones.

Caught

That fish must have been aghast
as I leaned in close over him,
smiling,
an odd black camera in my hands.

Look, see my reflection in his eye.

Eleven years old at the Arlington public pool,
a classmate thought it funny
to push my head under water
and hold it there.

I remember my wild thrashing,
my guttural panic
as I looked up at him
through blue water
and yellow sky;

the way he threw back his head
as he laughed;
the deep roof of his mouth;
his vicious horseshoe of teeth.

To My Doctors

yes, to *all* of you . . .
You need to know
that I want to give you
a chicken—
the biggest, most flamboyant
chicken ever seen.

I want to petition City Council
to change the homeowner codes
to let me raise chickens in the back
just to give one to you—

you, who saved my life;
who healed my body;
who made me whole again.

We are past the age of payments in coin
and almost dollars, and checks,
but this virtual transference of money
just doesn't seem adequate.

It's about the *gift*.

Now I'm sure you didn't go through twelve years
of medical school dreaming of poultry riches,
but I want to give you something big and vibrant
and squawking;

I want to watch your eyebrows rise
as it fills your grasp
and overflows your arms.

I want you to experience gratitude
in something so amazingly *alive*—
a wild beating heart
in your hands.

I Will Not Hide

The mammogram was Tuesday.
The biopsy, Wednesday.
I got the phone call Thursday.

I told the dog, fresh from the pound. He crawled
in my lap, reminding me *in hound* that he was *terminal*
just yesterday, reminding me miracles happen.

There was a band concert that night.
What did I used to think about on Thursdays?
I will not hide.

There was breast surgery. There was port surgery.
There was the first day at the oncologist, looking
at all the old bald women, who were looking at my hair—

waist long, catching on the arm of the chair. I wondered
if they knew how lucky they were to be 80 . . .
I will not hide.

I sat in that green recliner seven hours, week after week,
while skulls and crossbones dripped and
seeped in my veins. I will not hide.

I would not let my long hair fall, so I took it; *I took it;*
I shaved it *all.* And I was naked and vulnerable
and barren and scared,

but I took off my hat and tossed aside my wig;
and I walked the streets with my big, chunky
earrings, smiling so they'd wonder

if it was fashion or disease.
I will not hide.
I will say the word *cancer;*

I will tell you bald's the new black;
I will not hide. I will not hide.
Look me in the eyes. I will not hide.

Bitter Creek

—for James Duffy

We followed Bitter Creek
up the mountain.

All that was left of his vexed body
blazed down to ash
in a wooden box beneath her arm.

At just the right spot, we stopped,
the ridge of hills, a high bowl,
and us in the middle
with the good stuff—
the Buffalo grass,
yellow Rabbit Bush,
purple asters,
and the surprise of a white dog,

soaking wet,
his massive head in my hands,
gentle in manner,
eyes of amber,

and he laid his drenched body
at our feet
as we cut James out of the box,
out of the plastic bag;

everything strong about him
poured through the daisies
and the sage;

white dog always ten feet in front,
looking outward in each direction we turned
guardian of our simple sacrament.

The old ones speak
of the white spirit dog
who comes to carry departed souls
across the waters
to the afterlife.

Who are we to deny such myths,
when before us he sat
amongst September flowers,
circling like a patient moon,
wet as the River Styx.

And we held each other
as the wind piped low,
and the trilling grasshoppers
stitched the moments

till it was done—
a poem, a grief, a life;

white dog disappearing,
his deep horn bark
left to echo;
his long tail
trailing the waters behind.

Estate Sale

That night, we heard it,
the unmistakable cuttle of big cat,
the yelp of dying prey,
the great thump against cabin walls.

But it was night and wilderness,
where two-leggeds wait till light
to discover the fanged mess—
the bloody snow,
deer leg and torso,
paw tracks so massive
my outstretched hands fit inside.

For two days and nights they came,
in singles, in pairs;
Nature calling her own—
the Coyotes, the Coons,
the Beaver, the Chipmunks;

even Ravens drank the red snow,
Finches gathered fur for their nests;
all culling, sorting;
some hurried, some fighting,
some curious;

leaving nothing but the silence.
The natural progression
as each took their fill—
what they wanted, what they needed;
till finally the empty rooftop of ribs
was dredged away.

Down the street, old Mrs. Ryan's things
are stacked, tagged, perused.
I took two iron skillets,
one white porcelain teapot.

Perhaps Creation is its own afterlife;
the Deer becoming the Lion,
sprouting wings in the Raven;
an old woman's wisdom seeping into my belly
in tiny flecks of iron;

not one life lost
among the hanging branches
and cresting snows
and markers of stone,

even as bones are broken
and chewed and cindered,
or hollowed in the midday sun;

pale dust sifting back
into the great open mouth of the Earth.

What Has to Be Done

What are the odds
that the exact same seed pod
covered in mollusks
would appear on the beach
two days after I first found,
photographed,
and showed it to friends,
then hurled it as far as I could
back into the surf—to try to save it.

But there it was again, about a mile down.
So I took it home—the edges of the shells,
a bright orange . . .

the same colour as that feral cat
we trapped and took to the vet,
HIV positive,
and would infect the rest of the cats;

the one we had to put down—
that beautiful creature with his
long orange and white fur
and citrine eyes.

And we cried.

This sea pod won't return
to the ocean again—
the little lives long lost;

but I will say a prayer for all those
who have come and gone;
creatures that have crossed our paths,
fallen under our wheels,
or fed us when we hungered.

And although nature follows its stern course,
I promise you, there *is* a God of the great
and the small
who hears us when we weep;
who weeps Himself
as we speak gently to the dying.

CPSIA information can be obtained
at www.ICGtesting.com
Printed in the USA
FSOW01n0738110517
34107FS